THE
VIBRANT
TAPESTRY

Arti Sanjay Bangale

India | USA | UK

THE VIBRANT TAPESTRY

© 2024 Arti Sanjay Bangale

All rights reserved.

Presentation by *BookLeaf Publishing*

Web: www.bookleafpub.com

E-mail: info@bookleafpub.com

ISBN: 9789363314917

First edition 2024

PREFACE

This book is indeed a significant achievement for me. As my first published work, I am blessed and gratified to have completed it and to be able to share it with you. The idea for this book originated from a casual conversation with my father. He suggested that I share my original poems, and I agreed. Understanding the intricacies of publishing was challenging at first, but my father, my hero, was by my side every step of the way.

The title, "The Vibrant Tapestry," reflects a rich and colorful mix of experiences and emotions, much like a tapestry showcasing various hues and patterns. It evokes the beauty and complexity of life's different facets.

I hope you enjoy and appreciate the book.

This is the Future I See

This is the future I see of you and me,
Everything would have changed than it has to
be.

Things may have changed from the cradle to the
grave,
Only the bacteria may be alive because they are
brave.

Modifications would have been made with every
single thing,
Also nature would have shown its power for the
changes we have bring.

Technology would have bring people close but
not the hearts,
Also wars would have break the lands into many
parts.

Pollution would have reach it's highest peak,
But still the humans greed will continue to
streak.

So we will overcome this by keeping our
surroundings clean,
And making our world always healthy and
green.

Changing our future is in our hand,
So please be responsible before our successors
go and rant......

The Special Bond

Beyond the skies you reside there,
Just your mere presence and my sorrows
disappear.

Those tears rolling off mean everything to me
They are of happiness that I always meant to be.

This distance never seems a barrier when we are
joined by heart,
As leaves may fall off its branches but the roots
won't part apart.

You are the happiness over my sorrows, the
medicine for my every pain,
Just keep smiling more often and all my worries
will go in vain.

All the laughter we shared, the tears we wept,
For every affection we adore and the secrets we
kept.

It's in the comfort of a handhold tight,
And all beautiful dreams we had together every
night.

The most special bond without envy nor despise,
In all this forgery world you are my most trustful
disguise.

प्रकृति

आओ सारे करें हम प्रकृति की सैर आज
कितना है सुंदर देखो विश्व का यह ताज

इसमें हैं समाए देखो फल-फूल और पानी
हर पेड़ से सुनाई देती पंछियों की मधुर वाणी

हर समुद्र से सुनाई देती बहती लहरों की आवाज़
क्षण घुलती सूरज की किरणें बढ़ा देती हैं उनका साज़

अतरंगी बहती हवा देखो कैसे पेड़ों को झुलाए
पेड़ों में लटकते फल इससे कितना सुंदर दृश्य दिखाए

तो आओ सारे मिलकर हम संभाले रखें यह ताज
क्योंकि हमने ही छीनी है यह प्रकृति अपने अहंकार से
आज

कम कर दिए हैं पेड़ इसलिए कम हो रहा है पानी
अब तो बहुत कम बार सुनाई देती है पंछियों की वह
वाणी

कहाँ गए वो पेड़ जो देते थे सबको छाँव
और कहाँ गए वो तालाब, जिसमें धुल जाते थे सबके
घाव

अब नहीं रहे वो दिन जब सब रहते थे सुखद सु-भाव
और ना रही वह कोयल जो कु-कु कर रखती थी अपना
प्रभाव

कैसे हुआ यह सब ना तुम जनों ना हम
क्यों नहीं दिखाई देते हमे अन्य जीवों के वो गम

ना पेड़ों के दिखते अश्रु न प्राणियों की चीख
यह प्रकृति है सबकी हम सब के लिए यही है सीख।

Big brother

In the tapestry of life, a boy weaves his thread,
Sometimes sharp as a knife, yet from childhood,
he's bred.
He loves us fiercely, though his edges may cut,
In his heart, our bond remains, unblemished,
unshut.

He fights over silly things, like children often
do,
Yet beneath his bravado, lies a heart so true.
Strong and resilient, he stands in the storm,
A pillar of strength, his spirit, a form.

He bothers us incessantly, a sour lime's tart taste,
But in his actions, love's melody, not a waste.
His shouts may pierce the air, like thunder's roar,
Yet his presence, like wings, lifts us to soar.

In his contradictions, we find our own reflection,
A dance of light and shadow, a tender affection.
For in the depth of his being, we find our song,
In his presence, our hearts forever belong.

A citizen by Bapu's vision

In accordance with Bapu's vision, I pledge
To labor for a developed nation, my privilege.

A citizen of discipline, I vow to uphold,
Cleanliness and kindness, virtues untold.

In rebellion, Gandhi preached not violence's
sway,
For non-violence conquers all, come what may.

To develop ceaselessly, his call resounds clear,
In every heart, his legacy, dear.

I'll sway the world with simplicity's grace,
Bringing joy, not harm, in every place.

Uniting people in a formidable alliance,
Against any challenge, a resilient reliance.

For my nation's welfare, I'll tirelessly toil,
Not for self, but a collective soil.

Preserving ancient cultures, a sacred vow,
Spreading their essence far and wide, here and
now.

Assisting those in need, not just the wealthy,
Ending conflicts, fostering harmony stealthy.

Addressing inadequacies, with resolve unbent,
Rejecting complacency, to progress, I'm lent.

राह

चलता चला उस राह पर रुकना न तुझे आता है
जीवन का हर मोड़ हर वक्त कुछ नया सिखाता है।

सयम से चलने की शिक्षा विफलता तुझे देती है
और बढ़ता रह तू कभी न मुड़ना तेरी हिम्मत तुझसे
कहती है।

क्यों इस राह से डर रहा तू, यह तो तेरा साथी है
रुकना नहीं तू बढ़ते जाना, क्योंकि आगे तेरी आज़ादी
है।

माना की वो कड़कती धूप तुझे हर वक्त सताएगी
और हर कठिनाई में तुझे अपने परिवार की याद
आएगी।

पर तुझे न रुकना क्योंकि तू तो वक़्त है।
चाहे लाखों बाधाएँ आएँ तेरी कलम हर घड़ी सख़्त है

अंधेरी रातों में परिवार का साथ भी तुझे हर वक़्त
कमी दिलाएगा
पर अपनी माँ की वो डाँट याद कर तू खुद ही सो
जाएगा।

Teachers

Teachers' love, a boundless ocean's embrace,
A gift from above, enriching every space.

In classrooms of school or halls of college,
They impart wisdom, timeless knowledge.

Like trees adorned with leaves so green,
They nurture minds with visions keen.

Teachers, like atoms in life's grand design,
Fueling dreams, igniting minds to shine.

In the journey of learning, they lead the way,
Guiding steps through each passing day.

Their dedication, a beacon so bright,
Illuminating paths, dispelling night.

Let's cherish their love, let gratitude flow,
For teachers, like stars, help us grow.

Pandemic

This pandemic is spreading worldwide today,
From China's Wuhan, a virus is having its sway.

Corona, the name that's taking everyone's breath,
China has cunningly spread this deadly threat.

Everyone should stay at home, no one should go
out,
Because stepping out might be what Corona's
about.

But in this crisis, the poor are facing hunger
strife,
And laborers are walking because they want to
save their lives.

Doctors, police, and sanitation workers, like
gods, they stand,
Risking their own lives, saving everyone in the
land.

No shops are open now, no fields are free,
And if you meet someone, make sure a mask
you see.

Washing hands frequently is now a must,
And remember, maintain at least a meter's trust.

If someone comes, without washing hands, don't
let them in,
Even sanitize yourself thoroughly before you
begin.

If these precautions are followed, you can defeat
Corona's snare,
Because your and your family's safety is in your
care.

माँ

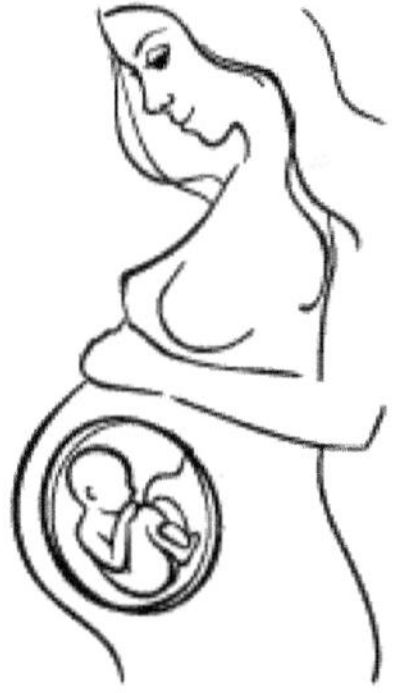

जो खुद रोए और हमे हँसाए,
जिसके एक स्पर्श से सब दुख मिट जाए।

जो जुटती रहे पर कुछ न कहे,
हम देखते रहे और वह जीवन भर कष्ट सहे।

जिसके होने से असतित्व है हमारा,
रात के अंधेरे में जिसकी गोद हमारे लिए सहारा।

वो तो भोली पर सबसे उत्कृष्ट है,
चाहे कितने भी बड़े क्यों न हो उसके लिए हर समय
हम कनिष्ठ है।

जिसने सहे सारे दर्द हमारे,
जिसकी आंखो के हम हैं राज-दुलारे।

जो खुद भूखी रहे पर हमे ज़रूर खिलाएँगी,
जीवन के हर पड़ाव में तुझे उसकी याद ज़रूर आएगी।

तो चलो उसे आज हम सब बताएँगे,
माँ, हम तेरा नाम रोशन करने के बाद ही घर आएंगे।

A little Rat

There once was a rat, quite plump and round,
Who stumbled upon a mat he found.
With a curious glance, he ventured near,
And settled comfortably, without any fear.

He curled up snugly, feeling quite grand,
On the soft mat, upon the land.
But as he dozed, so deep and sound,
He failed to notice the cat, sneaking around.

With a sudden pounce, the cat sprang forth,
Intent on catching the rat, of course.
But the rat, quick and nimble, dashed away,
Escaping the cat's claws for another day.

Through the cracks and crevices, the rat did flee,
To the safety of his burrow, where he'd be free.
The cat, frustrated, let out a hiss,
Knowing that for now, the rat had slipped its
kiss.

But the rat, now wiser, vowed to be more aware,
Of the dangers that lurked, both near and there.
For in this world of predators and prey,
Survival meant being alert, come what may

Memory

In the attic of my mind, where shadows dance,
Lies a treasure trove of memories, in a trance.
Each recollection a whisper from the past,
Moments woven in time, destined to last.

Through the corridors of my mind, I roam,
In search of memories, like gems in a tome.
Some gleam with the brilliance of the sun,
While others linger, like a forgotten one.

In the tapestry of my thoughts, they intertwine,
Moments of joy, sorrow, love, and wine.
They flicker like flames in the dark of night,
Guiding me through life's intricate flight.

Yet, some memories fade like stars at dawn,
Lost in the vast expanse, forever drawn.
But even as they vanish, they leave their trace,
Etched in the soul, in a sacred space.

So, let us cherish each memory we hold dear,
For they're the threads that weave our journey
clear.
In the symphony of life, they play their part,
Guiding us with their wisdom, from heart to
heart.

एकता की धारा

मैं रहता हर भारतीय के दिल में हूं, मैं तो अनमोल हूं,
मैं ही मृदु, मैं ही कठोर हूं, हर गगन पर मैं करता शोर
हूं।

मुझमें समाया पूरा मुल्क है,
सच्चे देशवासियों के लिए मुझसे आगे कोई शुल्क है।

खाकी वर्दी हो या ऊँचे मकान, हर जगह मैं लहराऊंगा,
अशुल्क भारत का अद्भुत सपना, मैं पूरा करके
दिखाऊंगा।

मिला था मुझे राष्ट्रध्वज का स्थान, सन् 1947 में,
पर आज स्वावलंभ से लहराऊँगा, हर घर में सन् 2022
में।

75 साल से था तो मैं असद के भाती पर अफसूर्दा में
रहता था,

और मेरे कारणवश तुम इनाद न करो, यह सबसे
कहता था।

उम्मीद थी कि इस साल तो हर घर तिरंगा
फ़रफ़राएगा,
और सच्चे अर्थ में यह स्वतंत्रता दिवस अमृत
महोत्सव कहलाएगा।

तो आओ इस वर्ष में तुम्हें तुमसे मिलवाऊँगा,
और हम सब अपनत्व से जीतेंगे, यह पूरे विश्व को
बताऊंगा।

बस गणतंत्र स्वतंत्र को नहीं, हर वक्त दिल में रखो,
यही अभिलाषा है,
और हर जाति में प्रेमत्व हो, यही हमारी देश भाषा है।

A letter to self

In the shadows where no light can dwell
Lies a darkness, a silent, haunting spell.
A weight that crushes, a void unseen,
Where despair reigns, in shades between.

In this realm where joy is but a dream,
Depression lurks, a relentless stream.
It steals the colors, paints life gray,
And whispers lies, in the mind's fray.

It wraps its chains around the soul,
Suffocates hope, takes its toll.
With every breath, a struggle deep,
In this abyss, where sorrows creep.

Yet in the heart of this bleak night,
A glimmer flickers, a spark of light.
For even in the depths of despair,
There's a strength, a resilience rare.

With courage as a guiding star,
We rise above, from shadows far.
We seek the dawn, embrace the day,
And find our voice, in our own way.

For though depression may cast its gloom,
Within us burns a sacred bloom.
A spirit fierce, a will to fight,
To reclaim our joy, our inner light.

Through tears we shed and battles fought,
We find the strength to rise, to be sought.
With love and support, we journey on,
Knowing we're never truly alone.

So let us reach out, extend our hand,
Together we'll rise, and firmly stand.
For in unity, there's strength to heal,
And in our stories, hope we'll reveal.

For every heart that's felt the ache,
Knows that light can pierce the dark's embrace.
And though the road may seem so long,
We'll find our way, with courage strong.

So let us walk, hand in hand,
Through valleys low, to heights, we'll ascend.
For in our struggles, we'll find our might,
And emerge from darkness, into the light.

Phoenix of Hope

In the chaos and the swirls of despair,
It may seem like the world's beyond repair.
When lives are shattered, dreams are undone,
The notion of hope can feel overrun.

But hold, dear heart, and don't lose sight,
For even in the darkest of nights,
Seeds of resilience silently sow,
A testament to how spirits grow.

Though destruction may rend and tear,
The world's end is not what we bear.
For from the ashes, new paths may rise,
Beneath the bleak, a sunrise lies.

It's in adversity that heroes are found,
In the rubble, courage does abound.
So let us rise, with strength unfurled,
For it's not the end of the world.

Together we'll rebuild, brick by brick,
With kindness as our mortar, love as our pick.
And though the scars may linger and twirl,
We'll find the light in this swirling whirl.

वसंत ऋतु

वसंत ऋतु है आया
फूलों की कलियों को फुलाया
हर तरफ हरियाली लाया
वसंत ऋतु है आया

हर बाग में फूल खिले हैं
हर वन मे मयूर नाच रहे हैं
हर पेड़ में छिपे घोंसले में
चूज़े खिलखिलाकर खेल रहे हैं

वसंत ऋतु है आया
सबके मन मे उत्साह जगाया
हर तरफ इस पवन पृथ्वी पर
टप-टप पानी बरसाया
वसंत ऋतु है आया

हर तरफ बरसात के पानी में
देखो कैसे नाव तैरती
बरसात अचानक आने पर
बच्चे कैसे झूम उठते

वसंत ऋतु है आया
सूखे पत्तो को हर रंग दिलाया
हर पेड़ मे उत्साह जगाया
वसंत ऋतु है आया
वसंत ऋतु है आया ....

Story of an aspirant

In the quiet depths where dreams take flight,
We lived as an aspirant, burning bright.
With hopes that soared on wings of grace,
We ventured forth to find our place.

Through trials and tribulations, we still strove,
With every setback, we held onto hope.
But shadows loomed in the path we began to
tread,
And doubts whispered, filling them with dread.

For every dream that slipped away,
Left scars unseen, in shades of gray.
And as we chased elusive stars,
We found ourselves trapped behind closed bars.

With each defeat, our spirit tried to wane,
And the fires within slowly drained.
The weight of failure, a heavy load,
This crushed our dreams, on the desolate road.

In the end, we stood alone,
Broken-hearted, our spirit prone.
For the journey we embarked upon,
Led us to a place where hope was gone.

Yet in our sorrows, a lesson learned,
That even in darkness, light can return.
For though our dreams may seem to fade,
A new dawn awaits, in the shadows' shade.

So here's to the aspirants, who dare to dream,
Though the path may be harsh, and not what it
seems.
For even in sadness, there's strength to be found,
As they rise from the ashes, to reclaim their
ground.

Guided by Wisdom

Today, life's tide, it sways and swells,
Atop the crest of wisdom's spells.

With knowledge's potion, we navigate,
Humanity's journey, saved by fate.

Through changing tides, we drift unknown,
Yet wisdom's light, our guide is shown.

Despite ignorance's destructive spree,
Knowledge reveals life's true decree.

From waters harnessed, a cup we fill,
The elixir of life, tranquil and still.

In changing times, questions arise,

But knowledge's medicine, our doubts it defies.

So onward we sail, with wisdom as an oar,
Through life's tempests, to a distant shore.

For in knowledge's embrace, we find our way,
Guided by truth, come what may.

गर्मियों की छुट्टियाँ

ग्रीष्म ऋतु का मौसम आया
छुट्टियों को भी संग लाया
भर पसीना ले कर आया
ग्रीष्म ऋतु का मौसम आया

अंतिम परीक्षा खतम हुई है
पूरा भोज तो निकल गया है
फिर भी दूसरे कंधे पर
बढ़ते साल का बोझ पड़ा है

ग्रीष्म ऋतु मे मिलेंगे सारे
नाना-नानी के राज दुलारे
पुस्तकों को न छुएँगे सारे
ग्रीष्म ऋतु मे मिलेंगे सारे

ना विद्यालय ना पाठशाला है
यह तो बच्चों का ज़माना है
खाए आम दिनभर सारे
क्योंकि सूर्य को भी जलाना है

बच्चे निकले कड़ी धूप में
ना कोई काम धाम रे
सूर्य भी लेता इनकी कठिन परीक्षा
क्योंकि उसको खाने को मिलता ना आम रे

ना सिर्फ खाना ना पीना है
ना सिर्फ बैठे रहना है
देश भर मे घूमे जाकर
क्योंकि इतिहास के पन्ने झांकने हैं

वीर शिवाजी जन्मे थे शिवनेरी की गोद में
तो शहंशाह की याद रहेगी ताज महल के योद में
तो आओ सारे घूमें जाकर इतिहास के बाग में
वीर पुरुषों की गाथाएँ देखें छुट्टियों के राग में

My Dad : My Hero

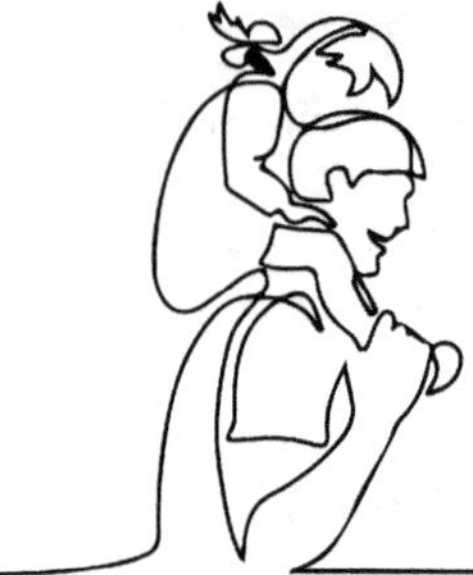

In every chapter of the book of my life,
There's one figure who shines amidst the strife.
A steadfast presence, a beacon so bright,
My father, whose love is my guiding light.

With hands that toiled and a heart so kind,
In his embrace, solace I always find.
Through laughter and tears, joy and pain,
His unwavering love forever reigns.

From childhood days to adulthood's embrace,
His wisdom and guidance I constantly trace.
He taught me to stand, to walk with pride,
In his footsteps, I found my stride.

In moments of doubt and moments of fear,
His words of wisdom always drew near.
With patience and care, he showed the way,
Through life's tumultuous display.

Through every challenge, every test,
His love and support, a constant quest.
In his strength, I found my own,
A bond between father and daughter, firmly
sewn.

As time unfolds its mysterious design,
His love for me, an unending line.
For in my heart, he'll forever reside,
My dad, my hero, my endless guide.

So here's to you, my father dear,
With gratitude and love that's sincere.
For all you've done and all you do,
My heartfelt thanks, I give to you.

Life

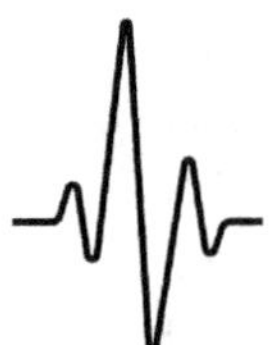

A life is like a park, its paths winding wide,
At times, veiled in shadows, where darkness may abide.
Yet amidst the gloom, there flickers a spark,
And through the densest night, there emerges a lark.

Sometimes, it's bathed in brilliance, so bright,
Where sunshine kisses each leaf in sight.
The laughter echoes, the joy takes flight,
As we dance in the warmth of the golden light.

Through the darkest hours, we find our way,
Guided by hope's faint and steadfast ray.
And when the dawn breaks, with its radiant might,
We emerge from the shadows, into the light.

So let us cherish the contrast, the hues,
For life's park is painted with myriad views.
In the dark and the bright, in the day and the night,
We find the essence of our journey's delight.

३७० धारा

भारत मे 370 धारा को मोदी ने निकाला है
अपने कर्तव्यों का पालन कर एक नया भारत बनाया
है

भारत के देश द्रोही को मोदी ने चौकाया है
कश्मीरी पंडितों के पुनर्वास से विश्वास जगाया है।

यह कहानी शुरू हुई थी जिन्हा के अहंकार की
भारत से पाक की कश्मीर के हिस्सेदार की

यह कहानी है कश्मीर के राजा हरीसिंघ की
उस समय कश्मीर न था भारत न पाक का

जिन्हा को चाहिए था कश्मीर पाक के सहयोग में
पर हरीसिंघ के मन में कश्मीर स्वतंत्रता के योग में

नेहरू के काष्ठों से आखिर कश्मीर भारत मे विलीन
हुआ
पर आज मोदी के निर्णय से सच्चे अर्थों से शामिल
हुआ

कहीं जवानों ने खाए पत्थर जो थे कश्मीर के तेनाथ
पर

अब यह नहीं होगा क्योंकि हट गया 370

अब गर्व से बोलो कश्मीर भारत की ही शान है
मुकुट के जैसे शिखर पर जो भारत का ईमान है॥

Rain therapy

In the wide expanse where gray clouds roam,
I find solace in rain's gentle home,
A therapy of nature's soothing grace,
Soft whispers on my upturned face.

Each drop descends, a tender kiss from above,
Healing touch, infused with divine love,
Easing worries, calming every pain,
In rain's embrace, I'm whole again.

Rhythmic beats, a tranquil symphony,
Nature's tears upon the earth, a remedy,
Cleansing heart and clearing weary mind,
In rain's therapy, peace I always find.

Embrace the storm, let it freely pour,
Washing away troubles to the very core,
In every drop, a renewal of the heart,
Rain's therapy, a balm to soothe every part.

Under the gray veil, nature's gentle caress,
A dance of renewal, a sweet tenderness,
Each raindrop a promise of new beginnings,
Washing away doubts and quieting the mind's
whisperings.

As raindrops weave stories upon the ground,
In their rhythm, serenity is found,
A melody of healing, a timeless art,
Rain's therapy, stitching together every torn part.

So I stand, under the soothing rain's sway,
Finding peace in nature's gentle display,
Embracing the storm, letting it cleanse my soul,
In rain's therapy, finding myself whole.

Draupadi's Cry

In the ancient halls where honor once held sway,
I stood, draped in destiny's unyielding play.
A queen of grace, yet fate's dice were rolled,
My dignity wagered, my story retold.

But tell me now, in this modern age's cry,
Do my tears mingle with every woman's sigh?
When my saree was torn by power's cruel might,
Was it just my voice that echoed in the night?

Oh, sisters of today, who face the silent gaze,
In boardrooms, streets, and tangled, endless
maze,
Do you feel the weight of centuries' scorn,
As history's shadows linger, unshorn?

Husband, warrior, and guardian of dharma's
light,
Why does your sword falter in the face of night?
Elders, wise and learned in justice's sacred lore,
Why does your silence echo, from shore to
distant shore?

Krishna, the charioteer of souls, divine and wise,
Do you watch as history's cycle endlessly ties?
In this age of progress, yet stained with old
strife,
Guide us to reclaim our honor, our life.

For in the echoes of my ancient lament,
I hear the cries of women, ceaseless, unbent.
Let this question pierce hearts like a sharpened
spear,
Till justice blooms, dispelling all fear.

In the silent whispers of each woman's cry,
Resounds the anguish of a thousand years gone
by.
Let us rise, united, in a fierce, defiant stand,
Till every woman's dignity is held in every hand.

Path to redemption

If within you, humanity lies dead,
Do not burden yourself on God's thread.

Wrap yourself in the shroud of introspection,
Bury the indifference, seek resurrection.

The message of God, elusive and profound,
Yet you turn away, deaf to its sound.

Wrap yourself in humility's embrace,
In humility find solace, in grace.

Heaven and hell, mere reflections of deeds,
Yet you abandon truth for fleeting needs.

For God's sake, let go of hollow pursuits,
Embrace virtue, abandon the pursuits.

How will you mend, by spreading fear?
The human heart, broken and seared.

Cease the cruelty, let kindness flow,
For God's sake, let compassion grow.

You, who slay innocence, heed this call,
Reflect on the tears, the sorrowful fall.

Have mercy on yourself, seek redemption,
For God's sake, embrace contrition.

If God's displeasure shadows your soul,
Respect His name, make your heart whole.

In reverence, seek the path of light,
For God's sake, awaken from the night.

Promise of Protection

She knows she is right, but cannot tell,
In silence, her wisdom does dwell.
She knows she deserves more, yet she refrains,
No blame to cast, no anger remains.

She understands what we never could,
Her depths, a mystery in womanhood.
Her heart holds truths we can't conceive,
In her presence, we learn to believe.

So, let us cherish, let us protect,
Her happiness is our utmost respect.
If we deserve freedom, why can't she?
Her spirit is boundless, wild, and free.

She is powerful, she is divine,
A reflection of us, in the grand design.

She carries burdens we may never know,
Yet through her strength, her beauty shows.

More precious than diamonds, her worth untold,
Her smile, a treasure more precious than gold.
Her laughter can light the darkest night,
In her joy, we find our own light.

Let's make a promise, a vow so pure,
To keep her safe, her joy ensured.
To lift her up when times are tough,
To remind her always, she is enough.

To keep her happy, to keep her secure,
For in her light, our love endures.
Together we stand, a promise to uphold,
To protect her spirit, fierce and bold.

For she is the heart of all that we are,
A guiding star, our shining par.
Let her dreams soar, her hopes ascend,
In her strength, our lives transcend.

So, let us cherish, let us protect,
Her happiness is our utmost respect.
In her power, in her grace,
We find our own sacred place.

Rainbow hoes of love

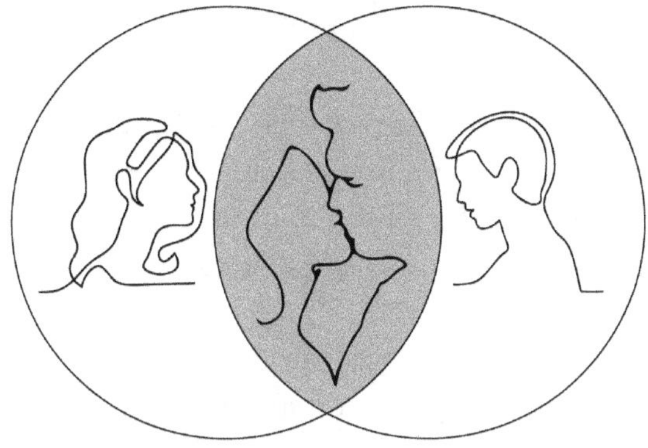

In colors of seven, you bloom, my love divine,
In every shade, you're the essence, so fine,
A shadow of my heart, forever intertwined,
Rainbow hues, our love defined.

Is there a light in you, why do you stay afar?
When you're close, I feel you, my guiding star,
Are you a dream or a fleeting shadow's trace?
In rainbow colors, your beauty I embrace.

This moment, where will the gentle breeze rest?
Love, not in force, but a fire, burning blessed,
It does not kindle by mere touch or spark,
Nor does it fade when put in the dark.

Your eyes, touched me with a gentle grace,
Softly, softly, my heart found its place,
A feeling awakened deep within my core,
You are the fragrance of life I adore.

Your breath, the essence of all that's true,
You are my desire, my longing for you,
In your warmth, my soul finds its ignite,
Your presence alone brings me to light.

I'm enchanted by your whispers, so sweet,
In silence, our eyes meet, secrets discreet,
I kneel before you, in reverence so deep,
Lost in your love, in thoughts that sweep.

In shadows of our hearts, forever entwined,
Rainbow hues, our souls forever aligned,
Is there a light in you, why do you shy away?
Near you, my love, emotions in rainbow array.

Lost in your path, entwined in your embrace,
Let me unravel, find solace in your grace,
Lost in your love, my senses entwined,
Lost in the passion of your love so kind.

My life, my breath, all consumed by you,
In passion, in love, my heart finds its true,
Now, no solace but in your embrace,
My life, my love, in your love, find grace.

You are the rainbow, in colors of seven,
You are my love, in every shade, heaven.

53

Krishna's whispers of peace

In the gentle whisper of the wind's soft song,
Krishna's voice echoes, steady and strong,
My child, release the burdens that you bear,
Trust in me, I'll shield you with loving care.

Let go of worries, let fears fade away,
I'll turn your night into the brightest day.
No weapon formed shall prosper, you'll see,
In my embrace, find peace and be free.

With perfect timing, I'll bless your days,
In the presence of foes, I'll light your ways.
Have faith, my child, in my eternal grace,
I'll lift you high, to a better place.

Hand over your heartache, let healing start,
For I am with you, forever in your heart.
Trust in me, my love will never part,
In every trial, find strength to restart.

In the silence of your prayers, I am near,

Listen closely, my voice is clear.
I am the solace in your darkest night,
Guiding you to dawn's golden light.

Through life's twists and turns, I'll be your
guide,
In every challenge, walk by your side.
The tears you shed, I collect with care,
Transforming pain into lessons rare.

Embrace the lessons, grow from the pain,
In every loss, find wisdom to gain.
For I am the source of endless love,
Showering blessings from above.

So surrender your worries, let them fly,
In my presence, you'll never be shy.
With unwavering faith, trust in my plan,
In my arms, find peace again.

In Krishna's words, a timeless embrace,
A symphony of love and grace.
Let his words echo in your soul,
Guiding you towards your ultimate goal.

Guided by the Gita: Paths to Enlightenment

Amidst the battlefield's chaotic roar,
Krishna's words, a beacon to explore,
Act with duty, with heart sincere,
Let go of outcomes, release your fear.

Paths to reach the soul's deep grace,
Through wisdom's light, or love's embrace,
In selfless service, find your way,
Let not desires lead astray.

Find peace in detachment's gentle sway,
Let go of cravings, find calm each day,
See divinity in every soul,
Beyond all differences that may toll.

Equal are we, in spirit's gleam,
Beyond the veil of life's grand scheme,
Face challenges with strength and might,
In every storm, seek inner light.

I am your guide, near and far,
With boundless love, like a guiding star,
Know yourself, find liberation's key,
In the depths of being, eternally free.

Thus spoke Krishna, in a timeless voice,
In the Gita's verses, hearts rejoice,
A path for humanity, brave and true,
To discover the essence of life anew.

The definition of eyes

The eyes that speak without a word, yet weep,
So strong, for every secret they keep.
They shimmer with joy, yet conceal the pain,
In silent whispers, they tell tales again.

They've seen the world in shades of light and
dark,
In their depths, lies the soul's tender spark.
Through tears and laughter, they silently convey,
The stories of hearts in their unique way.

In the quiet moments, their language profound,
They express what lips may never sound.
For in their gaze, emotions quietly reside,
The eyes, true windows, where secrets confide.

They care, they love, even show their rage,
Every emotion displayed on a beautiful stage.
In their depths, life's stories gracefully unfold,
Eyes, the silent narrators, brave and bold.

Through the veil of lashes, they watch and
observe,
With a gaze that can soften or sharply curve.
They witness the truth and perceive every lie,
Reflecting the soul, no mask to disguise.

In moonlit nights and sunlit days,
Their glimmering light guides lost ways.
They capture the essence of joy and sorrow,
Reflecting the past, present, and tomorrow.

They capture the essence of joy and sorrow,
Reflecting the past, present, and tomorrow.

Clinging to Fragile Hearts

Attachment scares me, friend or love,
A bond so deep, like skies above.

I don't get close to every soul,
Few touch my heart, make me whole.

When I attach, I give my all,
Two or three, and that's my call.

Their joy is mine, their pain, my tears,
Their smiles and cries, my hopes, my fears.

Their mood becomes the air I breathe,
Around their lives, my dreams I weave.

I build a world, a fragile place,
Terrified of empty space.

Anxiety, a shadow clings,
Replaced, forgotten, heartstrings' stings.

I'm still a child in love's sweet game,
No boundaries built, love's pure flame.

Like a child with a teddy near,
I give and give, despite the fear.

Yet in my heart, a longing stays,
To be loved back, in all the ways.

For bonds to me are life's bright art,
Unconditionally, from the start.

Sunshine's Embrace

After the quiet of the new moon's night,
A bright sunshine bursts forth with delight.
Golden rays dance upon the morning dew,
Chasing shadows, painting skies anew.

With warmth and hope in its gentle embrace,
Nature awakens with vibrant grace.
Fields and forests bathe in golden light,
As the world awakes from the peaceful night.

Birds sing praises to the day's first hour,
In the glow of sunshine's gentle power.
A symphony of life in morning's breeze,
Echoes the promise of peace and ease.

In the embrace of this radiant beam,
Dreams take flight, like a hopeful stream.
Underneath the azure, expansive dome,
Sunshine whispers of a new day's home.

Fragments of Farewell

In holding you close, I lost you forever,
I'm sorry for the wrongs, for the pain, however.
Thank you for being by my side till now,
This might be my last letter, words fail me
somehow.

Alone again, with no one to confide in,
Thank you for this loneliness, where I now
reside.
I accept defeat, my destiny's decree,
Memories haunt me, yet I must set them free.

I've never loved another as deeply as you,
Yet perhaps I was wrong, this truth is now true.
For all the love, the care, beyond my dreams,
I'm sorry for the hurt caused, it's more than it
seems.

It was my choice to start, and mine to end,
Please don't blame yourself, my dear friend.
Let's cherish those moments, let them be,
But release the pain, for you and for me.

Our bond once seemed the most beautiful of all,
But now I see, perhaps we were destined to fall.
I believed in us, in every word you said,
Yet now I wonder, were our dreams misled?

Forgive me for the changes that may come,
For the hurt they may bring, for all that's
undone.
I'm sorry for this time, for the path we must part,
Take care of yourself, heal your wounded heart.

Blossoms of new year

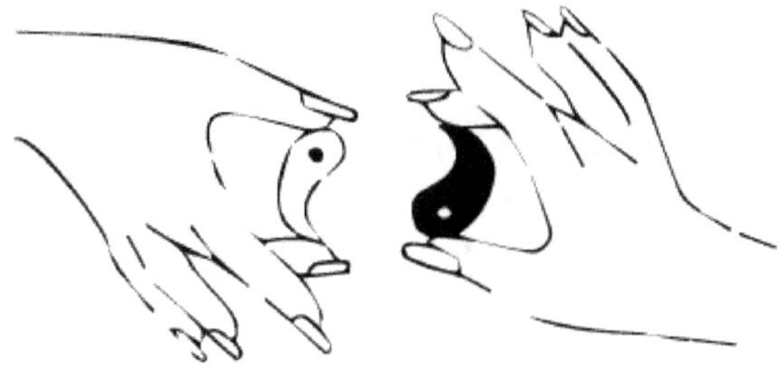

The year is about to end, my dear,
I hope the new one brings us cheer.
For us, our love, and our relation,
A fresh blossom, a sweet sensation.

This year was a wild, turbulent ride,
But it taught us to stay by each other's side.
Through dark times, we never parted,
Even when fights and jealousy started.

Let's carry this into the years ahead,
Promising to share our joy and dread.
Though time is fleeting, moments few,
It's not about time, it's about me and you.

So here's to a New Year, my everything,
May our love continue to brightly sing.
Six days till the year's end, Christmas here,
I know we can't be together, my dear.
We need each other now, but alas,

Reality strikes, and time must pass.
It's okay we're not next to each other,
Our hearts stay warm, despite the bother.

Next Christmas, we'll miss the hand-in-hand,
But our love's warmth will forever stand.
Let's start this new year with a vow,
To never part, no matter how.

I wish upon Santa, the stars so high,
For our love to last and never die.
Here's to resilience, to our fight,
May the New Year keep our love alight.

In the darkest times, we stood strong,
Fighting over silly things, yet never wrong.
Through highs and lows, our love has grown,
A testament to the bond we've shown.

Let's promise to never stray apart,
To share our joys and every heart.
Though we're together for moments brief,
Our love will conquer every grief.

So a very Happy New Year, my everything,
With you, my heart will forever cling.
To us, my dear, to love so bright,
May our future be filled with light.

A flicker in the dark

Beneath a sky of somber gray,
A girl fights through another day,

Weary of the endless fight,
In shadows, searching for the light.

Parents, friends, and kin combined,
Their voices blend, a tangled line,

Each expectation, pressure, strain,
Adding to her silent pain.

Her heart, though tired, still beats on,

A whispering hope, a fragile song,

In darkest nights, a flicker bright,
Believing dawn will break the night.

She dreams of peace, a gentle place,
Where burdens lift, and fears erase,

And in her soul, a spark ignites,
A promise that the world turns right.

With every breath, she holds this truth,
A strength within, a seed of youth,

For in her heart, despite the storm,
A hope endures, a love reborn.

Solitude's Lament

When someone met me, it felt so grand,
My world turned to songs, as if planned.
Colors rained and fragrance blew,
The air now scented, skies anew.

Winds intoxicated, directions gone,
Gestures changed, a new dawn.
Hopes awakened, heartbeats swift,
Breaths stormed, lips with melodies swift.

Dreams in eyes of moments past,
When someone came, and shadows cast.

How to tell, how it began,
Love spread with locks unplanned.

Like behind fog, a dew-kissed flower,
A moon in clouds, peeking hour by hour.
Eyes bright with morning's glow,
A dream sea, with love stars aglow.

Waves talking, pearls showering,
Silver anklets jingling, hearts flowering.
Glass goblets falling, a sitar played,
Moonlit songs softly swayed.

Sweet talks, meetings brief,
Melting hearts, desires in relief.
Moon descends, earth embraced,
Heaven here, no dream misplaced.

He called, explained our fate,
Meant to meet, flowers' bloom innate.
Lifetimes' bonds, lifetimes' ties,
Each birth, we meet under the skies.

Honeyed whispers in my ear,
Dreams' doors opened, visions clear.
Dreamworld so beautiful and bright,
Colorful realms in the night.

But dreams broke, eyes awoke,
Consciousness returned, truth spoke.
The one who came, and shadows cast,
Entered heart, now in the past.

Heart now lonely, desires gone,
No more dreams to carry on.
Days and nights filled with tears,
Talks of pain and lamenting years.

No one left, just me, and memories,
Of lost love, whispers in the breeze.

Echoes of Climate

Beneath the relentless gaze of the sun,
Earth whispers a sorrowful tale, undone.
Glaciers, once mighty, now weep in silent
streams,
Their tears trickling into oceans, fueling
warming dreams.

Oceans rise with restless, mournful tides,
Where coral reefs, vibrant homes, now hide.
Icebergs in the Arctic, majestic and cold,
Melt into memories, a story of worlds untold.

Forests ignite in flames of despair,
Leaving scorched earth and ashes bare.
Species fade into the dusk, their echoes fading
fast,
In the aftermath of choices, where time slips
past.

A polar bear's haunting cry pierces the air,
Her cubs weak, the ice beneath their feet rare.
Their kingdom of white, a vanishing tale,
Lost to warming seas and winds that wail.

Cities swelter under the unforgiving sun,
Concrete jungles pulse, but green spaces run.
Children play with masks, their innocence at
hand,
Breathing air thick with regret, across the land.

Yet hope lingers amidst the haze and heat,
In the hearts that beat, in the hands that meet.
Together, we can rewrite our fate,
Mend the Earth, before it's too late.

The Trident of Infinity

O Lord Shiva, in the stillness of the cosmos'
breath,
Where stars are but whispers of the void,
I see you standing, sovereign and serene,
Divine Mahadev, the ever-poised.

With your trident, you wield the force
Of creation, preservation, and decay,
In your cosmic dance, you chart the course,
Balancing night and day in a divine way.

O gracious Lord, hear my humble plea,
*Guide me with your wisdom, set my spirit
free.*
Your third eye, O mighty One,
Illuminates beyond the veil of time,

Your gaze pierces through the boundless night,
Unraveling the mysteries, sublime.

Mount Meru's whispers, the Ganges' gentle
flow,
All bow before you in reverence and awe,
In deep meditation, your presence shows,
The eternal truths, the sacred law.

O compassionate One, grant me your light,
Illuminate my path, turn darkness to bright.
Your matted locks, adorned with the moon's
crown,
Waves of ash marking your timeless grace,

From your stillness, you roar, the universe's
sound,
In the silence, you reveal the sacred space.

O bearer of the Trident, guide me through the
expanse,
Your infinite form defies all ends,
In every breath, I sense your cosmic dance,
To you, O Lord, with humble heart, I bend.

O Lord, bless me with your eternal flame,
In your divine presence, I find my aim.
For in your trident, I see the infinite,
The endless cycles, the eternal flame,

The essence of all that is and shall be,
Shiva, I chant your sacred name.

In the stillness of the cosmos' breath,
I find your presence, ever so divine,
O Lord of Shiva, conqueror of death,
To you, my soul I do consign.

The Dream That Wasn't Meant to Be

With a tender heart, I watched my wildest dreams take flight,
But as youth arrived, my dearest vision faded from sight.

A thought without forgery, pure as the morning dew,
I held onto that dream, believing it would come true.

But destiny played its game and made it worse,
Turning my cherished hopes into a silent curse.

As I grow old, the truth becomes clear to me:
This was never a dream that was meant to be.

Still, I labored to preserve it with all my might,
Yet every effort faltered as new duties came to
light.

Responsibilities weighed heavy, dimming the
gleam,
And the dream I once cherished became a
fleeting dream.

In the twilight of my days, I see the truth unfold,
That some dreams are fleeting, never meant to
hold.

With a wistful heart, I accept this reality,
The dream that wasn't meant to be, has finally
set free.

Phantoms of the Mind

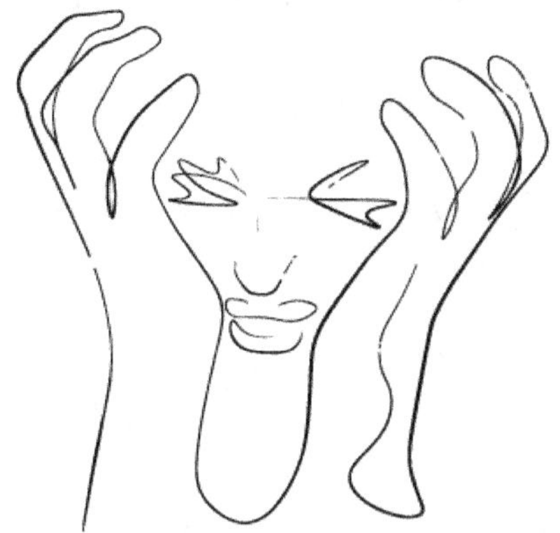

In the stillness of the night, phantoms softly
creep,
And no one was present when you wept in deep.

You can't make efforts to trust, for even a
fleeting thought,
Brings back the pain, worsening every battle
you've fought.

You never asked for it, but it was destined to be,
A relentless shadow, forever haunting thee.

You tried to get over those dark traumas and
fears,
But they lingered still, through the passing years.

And you kept them hidden, veiled from all who
cared,
Assuming they'd blame you for actions you
hadn't dared.

In solitude, you faced what you couldn't share,
A silent struggle, while no one else was aware.

When you tried to tell them, they didn't believe
it was true,
And when you tried to explain, their doubts only
grew,

Fearing that their judgments would be too harsh
to face,
You withdrew in silence, finding solace in space.

Your journey was tough, yet you held your own
pace,
With strength in your heart, you faced every
challenge with grace.

Believing the traumas won't haunt you anymore,
Finding peace within, and strength to restore.

Gratitude's Radiant Path

As gratitude's radiance guides each step anew,
Yet we try to refrain from what is true.

We have shelter, we have food to eat,
Yet we often overlook these blessings so sweet.

Taking it for granted as if it is endless,
Blind to the beauty in life's small, tender caress.

In moments of doubt, when shadows cast their shade,
The light of thankfulness helps us to wade.

The nature has its limits, even if we are greedy,
A reminder that abundance isn't always easy.

We should embrace the blessings we've been
given so freely,
For they are the jewels that make our lives truly

Thanking for the breath we breathe each day
with grace,
In every moment, let gratitude fill our space.

Respecting it with all the devotion we can trace,
Making efforts to not let it disappear from our
space.

With each act of gratitude, we brighten our
place,
And find our true wealth in life's warm embrace.

Let us cherish the moments, both big and small,
For in gratitude's light, we find the strength to
stand tall.

In every sunrise and every sunset's glow,
May our hearts be open to the love we bestow.

Branching Hearts

From deep-rooted love, our branching hearts
flourish,
In the garden of family, where beautiful
memories nourish,

May it have been dark, may it have been bright,
Our bond endures, steadfast through day and
night.

Each connection, a commitment of love, not
fleeting,
In the warmth of our bond, no moment's worth
defeating.

Yes, sometimes clashes occur, yet our bonds
remain strong,
For family is where every heart finds where it
belongs.

Like our five fingers, though different, form a
fist,
Together we stand, in unity's strong, enduring
mist.

Remembering those juvenile smiles and also the
youthful cries,
We see time's passage in the wisdom of our
parents' eyes.

As we navigate life's twists, we embrace our
shared fate,
Grateful for the moments before it's too late.

Through trials and triumphs, our love remains
grand,
A testament to the strength of a united, enduring
band.

In every laugh, every tear, our hearts resonate,
In the family's embrace, we find our truest state.

Through each season's change, our roots grow
deep,
In the garden of family, love is ours to keep.

We cherish the lessons and the bonds that we've
grown,
In the tapestry of life, our hearts have always
known.

With every challenge faced, our love only
expands,
In the sacred unity of our entwined hands.

With deep admiration, we honor the ties we
create,
For in this sacred bond, our souls perpetually
celebrate.

Across the Miles, Heart to Heart

Though distance stretches wide and far,
Our hearts remain close under the same star.
I knew it was not easy, this journey we tread,
With miles between us and dreams overhead.

Yet in every challenge, our bond only grows,
Through whispers of love and the hope that it
shows.
In the silence between our words, emotions
speak their heart,
And we cherish the trust that plays its crucial
part.

Though misunderstandings came, we learned to
cope with grace,
For our love and commitment always found its
place.
Dreams of our reunion keep our spirits bright,
Guiding us gently through each lonely night.

Memories we treasure, moments we hold dear,
Echo through the distance, bringing you near.
Letters and calls, our lifelines they became,
In every word and phrase, we whisper each
other's name.

The days may be long, the nights often cold,
But thoughts of our future make us bold.
We count down the moments until we reunite,
When our separate paths converge in the light.

Until that day comes, we stay strong and true,
With faith in our hearts, we'll see it through.
For love knows no bounds, no matter the miles,
And our hearts remain close, under shared skies
and smiles.

Moonlight in a Shattered World

In the moon's soft caress, gentle light reveals,
A tender touch that the darkness heals.
Yet as shadows loom and chaos swirls,
We wonder if this is the end of the world.

Though love persists through the night's soft
glow,
Distance grows where our hearts should flow.
In a world undone, where we drift apart,
Can we mend the rift that tears at our hearts?

As the moon casts its light on our fractured fate,
We search for solace, though it's growing late.
In the quiet of the night, beneath its watchful
gaze,

We hope for a dawn to end these troubled days.
For in the moon's light, we find a fleeting peace,
A glimpse of tomorrow where our wounds might
cease.
Until then, we wander through this shadowed
strife,
Guided by moonlight, seeking meaning in our
life.

The stars above, in their distant dance,
Offer a promise of a second chance.
In their shimmering light, we dream and yearn,
For a world where the tides of chaos might turn.

Through the night's embrace, as we seek to
mend,
We hold to the hope that hearts can transcend.
For though the world may shatter and bend,
In moonlight's grace, our spirits ascend.

And when the moon's light fades with dawn's
first gleam,
We'll carry its warmth through our waking
dreams.
With every tear and every silent plea,
The moon's tender glow will guide us to be free.

The Intersection of Mind and Divinity

In the dawn of intellect, where shadows conflate,
A mind embarked upon a quest, driven by fate.

From primordial embers to celestial beams,
He pursued the essence beneath every dream.

In ancient murmurs of cosmic chance,
He discerned the divine in the mystic dance.

The deities and legends, in sanctuaries
enshrined,
Revealed a universe both arcane and refined.

Scriptures and tomes from epochs afar,
Unfurled narratives of faith, profound as a star.

Through rites and prayers, he aspired to the
divine,
Seeking immutable truths in the cosmic design.

Then emerged an era where reason ascended,
In laboratories where light and inquiry blended.

Atoms fragmented and the cosmos unfurled,
In the realm of science, the enigmas swirled.

Yet amid empirical quests and veiled haze,
He perceived the sacred in the scientific maze.

In the vast expanse, where stars intertwine,
He glimpsed ancient deities in the grand design.

At the confluence where paths of knowledge
converge,
He discovered harmony where science and spirit
merge.

For the evolution of man, profound and grand,
Weaves together the old and the new with an
enduring hand.

Whispers in the Quiet Room

In a quiet room, where shadows play,
A book and a smartphone lay.
The book, with pages soft and worn,
Whispered of days when it was born.

It spoke of nights by candle's gleam,
Where every word held weight and dream.
'Once, I was the keeper of thoughts,
In ink and paper, I wove the knots.'

The smartphone, silent in its glow,
Carried a world it couldn't show.
Yet, in its presence, a quiet hum,
Of knowledge vast, of things to come.

The book continued, soft and slow,
'In my stillness, truths do grow.
Each page turned by a careful hand,
Reveals a world, both vast and grand.'

The smartphone, though without a voice,
Seemed to respond, as if by choice.
'I hold the world in every scroll,
A digital path to every goal.'

But as they lay side by side,
In the silence where stories abide,
There seemed no conflict, no need to choose,
For both had value, both had use.

One spoke of history, old and wise,
The other of futures yet to rise.
Together they rested, each with a place,
In the endless journey of the human race.

The Butterfly of Hope

In the hush of dawn, where dreams ignite,
A butterfly flutters, soft and light.
With wings of shimmering, delicate hue,
It dances on whispers of morning dew.

It flutters through moments of meeting new,
Bringing hope like petals kissed by the dew.
In the meeting of eyes, a spark, a flame,
The butterfly whispers, 'There's no shame'

It flutters through dreams, both distant and near,
Turning visions of grandeur crystal clear.
In the chase of a goal, the heart's true aim,
The butterfly murmurs, "You'll find your name."

It soars on the currents of happiness found,
Through laughter and joy, where hearts abound.
In the simple moments of bliss so pure,
The butterfly sings, "This love will endure."

In the crowded spaces where silence calls,
It finds peace in the midst of life's grand halls.
Amidst the chaos, where solitude might roam,
The butterfly whispers, "You're never alone."

When shadows fall and the spirit feels weak,
It wraps its wings around the courage you seek.
In the lowest of lows, where strength feels thin,
The butterfly's breath says, "You will win."

So, let the butterfly of hope take flight,
Guiding you through the darkest night.
With dreams to chase, and love to hold,
Its wings will carry you, brave and bold.

Why Seek Sorrow?

In the heart's deep well, where shadows dwell,
Magic swirls in the air's gentle spell.
The dawn eludes not where night once reigned,
For ecstasy blooms where moonlight is framed.

Dreams are woven not with tear-stained eyes,
But in the vast expanse where vision flies.
Solace is found not in the crowd's disguise,
But in the grace that even strangers can provide.

Daylight's pursuit where darkness claims,
Is met with moonlit paths, where rapture flames.
Tears that fall reveal truths profound,
In their cascading dance, wisdom is found.

On the road of desires, wonder not,
For rain falls softly where you have sought.
And the morning that renews youth's gleam,
Is a radiant tome, a brilliant dream.

Embrace the freedom life bestows,
Why confine yourself where dimness grows?
Joy is not where darkness lays its claim,
But in the moon's embrace, where light remains.

The Cage of Contemplation

In the quiet chambers of a restless mind,
Thoughts swirl in a maze, unkind.

Questions echo in the dim-lit hall,
Where every choice seems to rise and fall.

She wonders if love's gentle face,
Holds truth or just a fleeting trace.

Is the heart's desire, so deeply known,
A guiding light or a shadow thrown?

Career paths stretch in a tangled snare,
With dreams that shimmer, but haze and glare.

Will effort and ambition carve a way,
Or fade in the dusk of an uncertain day?

Happiness dances in a distant gleam,
A promise of joy, a cherished dream.

Will it linger, or swiftly pass by,
Leaving only echoes of a hopeful sigh?

The mind, a prison of doubt and fear,
Weighs each choice with an invisible tear.

In the chase for what's right, and what's true,
She's bound by the "what ifs" that ensue.

Yet within this cage of ceaseless thought,
Lies the strength that she's long sought.

For through the confusion and the night's
shroud,
A glimmer of hope, fierce and proud.

She'll find her path through the inner storm,
Where love and success take their true form.

In the prison of her mind's design,
Freedom will come, as stars align.

In the Moment's Whisper

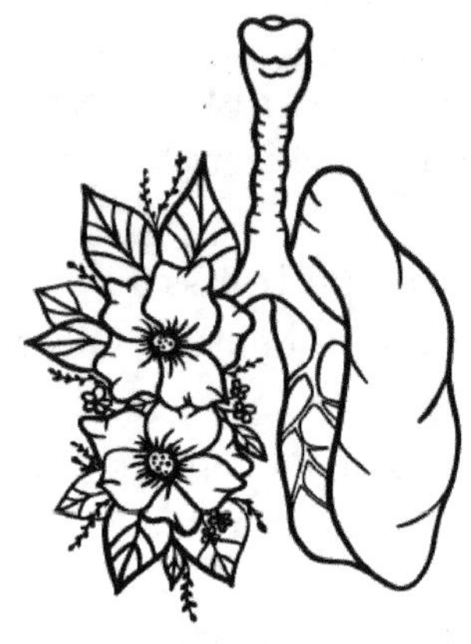

A golden ray cuts through the morning mist,
Warming your face with a gentle kiss.

Did you welcome its light or let it stray,
Lost in the shadows of a weary day?

A vibrant bloom in the garden sways,
Its colors bright in the sun's warm gaze.

Did you linger to admire its grace,
Or hurried past in the frantic race?

A child's laughter, pure and clear,
Transforms the day with joy sincere.

Did you share in the mirth or let it pass,
Wrapped in worries that seemed too vast?

Birds chirp softly as dawn breaks free,
Their melody dancing on the breeze.

Did you pause to hear their morning song,
Or let it fade as you moved along?

A breeze drifts softly through open space,
Offering comfort with its cool caress.

Did you notice its touch or miss its tune,
Burdened by troubles that loomed too soon?

In each fleeting moment, beauty lies,
A spark of joy beneath the skies.

Did you cherish these gifts as they came your
way,
Or let them slip by in the fray?

In the Mirror's Gaze

In the quiet of night, when shadows play,
She wonders why her heart gives so much away.

Offering warmth to the cold and the lost,
Yet finding her own soul comes at a cost.

Why does the kindness she freely imparts
Leave her with echoes and aching hearts?

In a world where love is often withdrawn,
She smiles through tears at the break of dawn.

Her family, the closest, often feels distant,
Anger erupts where affection is consistent.

Why does her wrath flare in moments of need,
When their presence should be a balm, not a
seed?

Though she's cast aside for her gentle ways,
Her spirit endures through the longest days.

In the mirror's gaze, there's a truth she sees,
That kindness is not always met with ease.

Her heart, a beacon in the darkest night,
Guides the lost with its enduring light.

Though others may falter and hearts may turn,
Her essence remains, an eternal burn.

She continues her journey, despite the pain,
With a heart that gives, and a soul that's lain.

For in the act of giving, she finds her grace,
A light that shines in an empty space.

Poetic reverie

In the realm of words, where emotions freely
flow,
Poetry thrives, an artistry we cherish and know.

From the fusion of dreams and thoughts
untamed,
Springs forth poetry, in rhythmic beauty framed.

Like a tailor stitching tales with delicate thread,
Or a cobbler crafting shoes for paths we tread,

Poets weave emotions, deep and true,
Giving voice to sentiments old and new.

In the whisper of an idol's distant voice,
We find the truth, in poetry's rejoice.

To be human is fate, but to be a poet, rare,
A blessing that transcends, beyond compare.

Not made, but born, with a gift so grand,
Poetry breathes life, across every land.

For a poem isn't judged by good or bad,
It simply exists, a reflection of emotions we've
had.

A poet dreams of verses yet to be penned,
By another's hand, where their hopes transcend.

To see their thoughts and feelings embraced,
In a tapestry of words, perfectly placed.

Wishing for a line, a stanza, a rhyme,
That captures their essence, across space and
time.

A legacy of dreams, both cherished and rare,
Immortalized in poetry, with beauty to spare.

In this world of verses, where hearts confide,
Poetry lives on, a treasure we hold inside.